Worst Things About the Internet

Catherine Rondina

Series Editor
Jeffrey D. Wilhelm

Much thought, debate, and research went into choosing and ranking the 10 items in each book in this series. We realize that everyone has his or her own opinion of what is most significant, revolutionary, amazing, deadly, and so on. As you read, you may agree with our choices, or you may be surprised — and that's the way it should be!

an imprint of

SCHOLASTIC

www.scholastic.com/librarypublishing

A Rubicon book published in association with Scholastic Inc.

Associate Publishers: Kim Koh, Miriam Bardswich
Project Editor: Amy Land
Editor: Jessica Rose
Creative Director: Jennifer Drew
Project Manager/Designer: Jeanette MacLean
Graphic Designer: Doug Baines

The publisher gratefully acknowledges the following for permission to reprint copyrighted material in this book.

Every reasonable effort has been made to trace the owners of copyrighted material and to make due acknowledgment. Any errors or omissions drawn to our attention will be gladly rectified in future editions.

"Stolen Lives: Identity Thief Finds Easy Money Hard to Resist" (excerpt) by Tom Zeller Jr., *The New York Times*, July 4, 2006.

"Caught in the Web" (excerpt) from "Video game addiction all too real" by Katherine Nguyen, *The Orange County Register*, January 28, 2007.

"A Victim's Story" (excerpt) from "Cyberbullying" reported by Joan Leishman, produced by Lani Selick and Alison Hancock, CBC.ca, October 10, 2002.

Cover image: All Images–Shutterstock

Library and Archives Canada Cataloguing in Publication

Rondina, Catherine
The 10 worst things about the Internet / Catherine Rondina.

Includes index.
ISBN 978-1-55448-556-7

1. Readers (Elementary). 2. Readers—Internet. I. Title.
II. Title: Ten worst things about the Internet.

PE1117.R66 2007 428.6 C2007-906886-3

2 3 4 5 6 7 8 9 10 10 17 16 15 14 13 12 11 10 09 08

Printed in Singapore

Contents

File Edit View History Bookmarks Window Tools Help

SYSTEM FAILURE

Without a doubt, the Internet is one of the greatest inventions of all time. Where else can you see artwork from museums in countries around the world, find information on just about anything, and chat with your friends — all simply by typing a few words on your keyboard? But despite all of these benefits, the Internet also has its share of problems.

The Internet can be a place where sneaky criminals hide out. They use their superb computer skills to steal money or to crack computer codes to cause major damage! Other problems with the Internet can cause emotional or physical pain — pain that can take years to heal.

In choosing and ranking the 10 worst things about the Internet, we considered the following: the damage caused; the number of people affected; whether the damage can be fixed; and whether it can be prevented.

So before you get caught in the Web, try to decide:

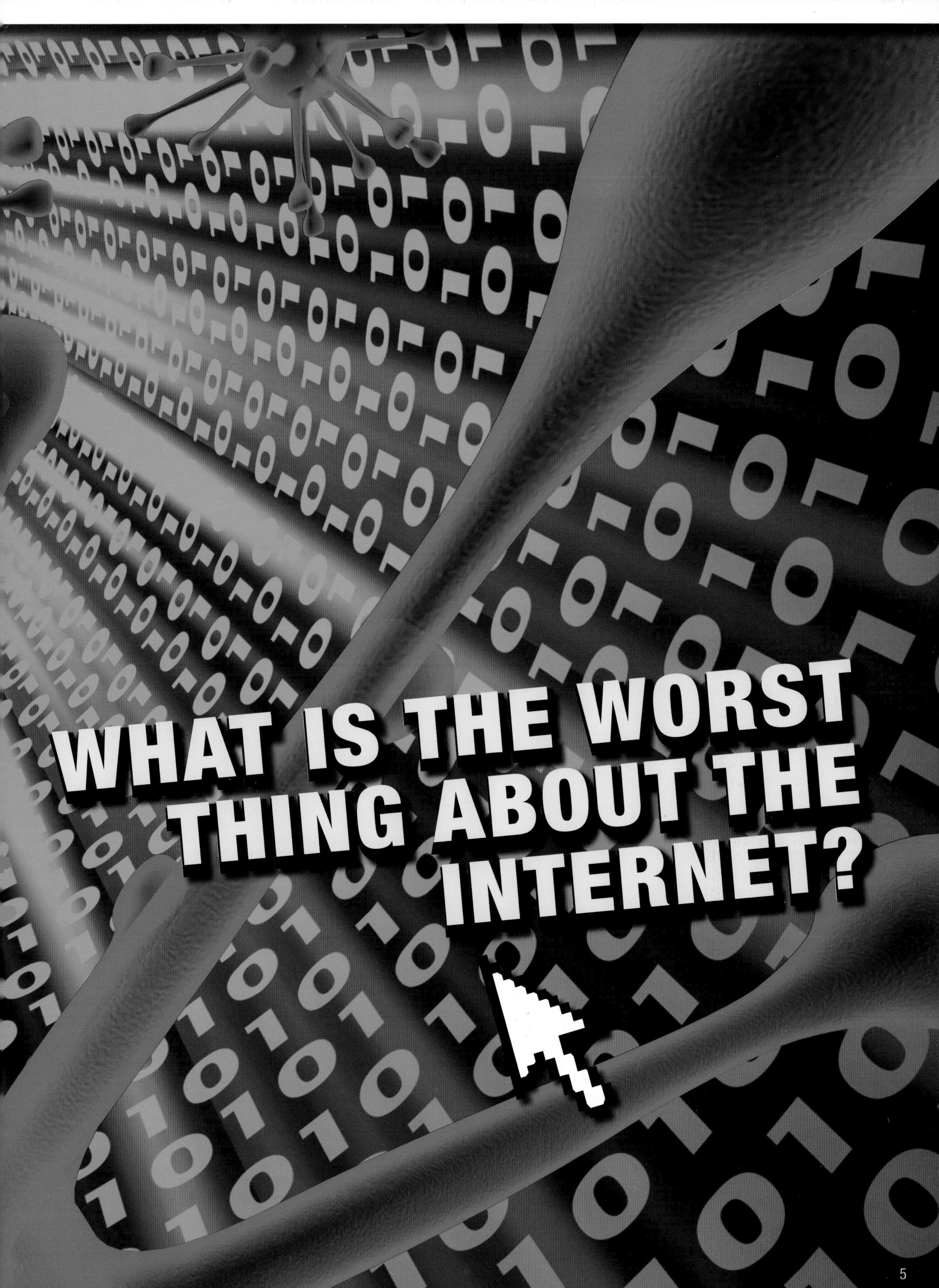
WHAT IS THE WORST THING ABOUT THE INTERNET?

10 BAD ERGONO

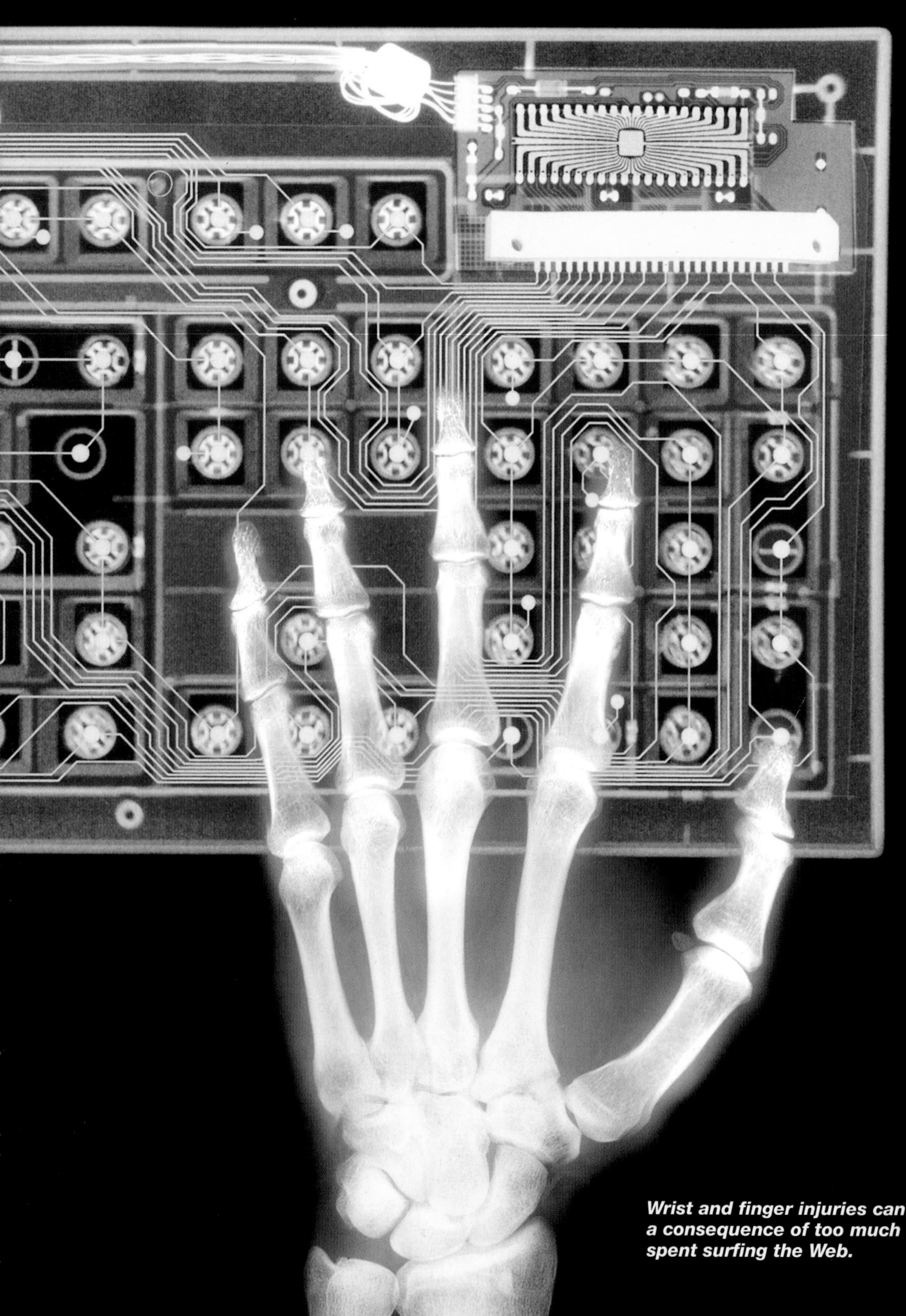

COMPUTING X-RAY–© LESTER LEFKOWITZ/CORBIS

Wrist and finger injuries can be a consequence of too much time spent surfing the Web.

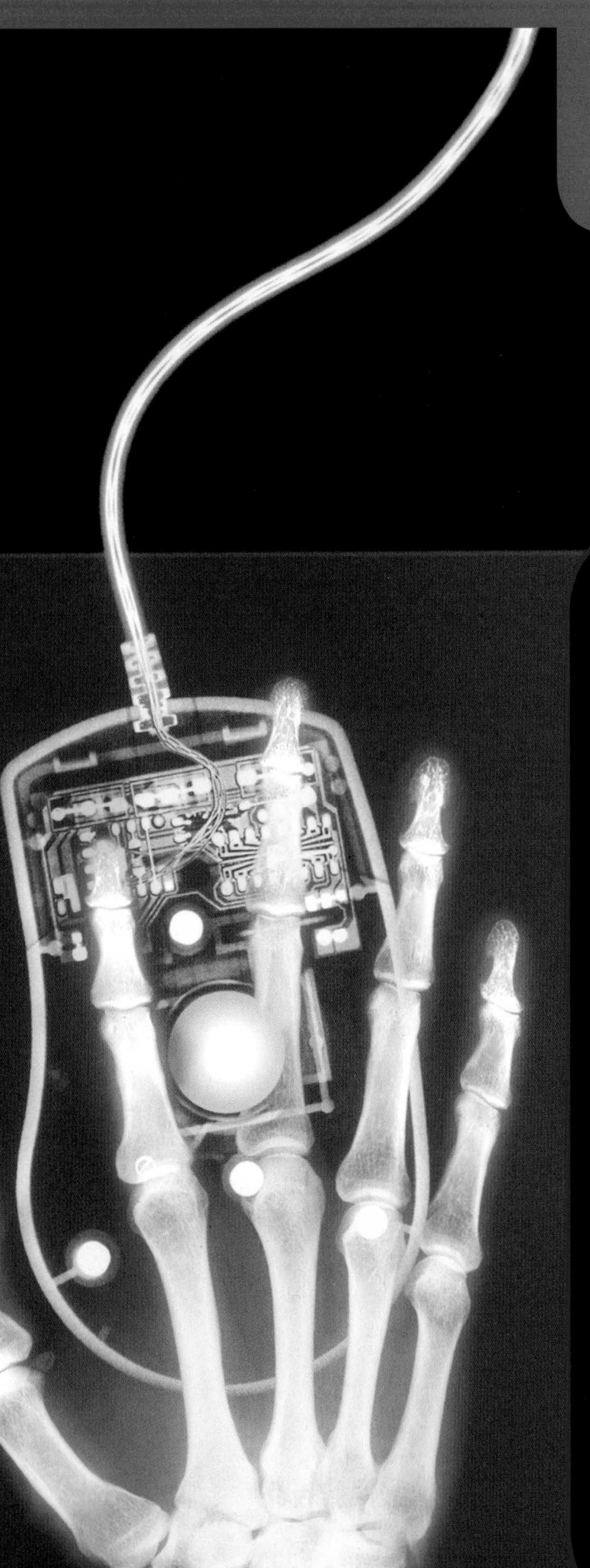

ALSO KNOWN AS: The science of equipment design

NET NIGHTMARE: Computer-related injuries can happen at any age, but for bodies that are still developing, the damage could last a lifetime.

Sitting at your computer all day can be more than just a pain in the neck! Spending hours surfing the World Wide Web can also strain your eyes, cause damage to your back, and hurt your wrists and hands. There is even a possibility that some of these injuries might become permanent.

Ergonomics is the science of setting up a work station so that it is comfortable and efficient. This is very important since time flies when you're having fun! It's easy to spend hours playing online computer games or visiting your favorite Web sites. Since many Internet users forget to take breaks, it is important that desks and computers are set up properly. This includes making sure that monitors are at eye level and that chairs are designed for good posture.

Poor ergonomics might not sound too scary, but this painful problem can lead to damage that can cause years of discomfort and even require surgery!

BAD ERGONOMICS

Users should keep their wrists straight, position the screen so its top is at eye level, and use chairs that give firm support to their lower backs.

TECH MESS

Daily computer use can cause physical harm to the body. This has chiropractors very worried! Many predict that misuse of computers will lead to a rise in health problems for the current generation of young computer users. Young people are spending more time sitting in one place than they ever have before.

Do you think that there is such a thing as spending too much time on the Web? Explain.

SO WHAT?

Anybody who spends a lot of time in front of a computer is at risk for a number of medical consequences. One of these risks is carpal tunnel syndrome. This is a very painful and often permanent wrist injury. It can be caused by repeated movements, such as typing, which can damage a nerve in the wrist. Another common injury caused by bad ergonomics is back pain. This is due to poor posture. Also, dry eyes can be a side effect of staring at a computer screen for too long. This can cause blurred or double vision, which can be permanent.

---

chiropractors: *health care professionals who specialize in treating skeletal and nervous systems*

FIGHTING BACK!

Luckily, there are ways to protect yourself from computer-related injuries. Start by adjusting your chair so that your feet rest flat on the floor. Also, position your computer screen so that the top of the monitor is at or below your eye level. This will help to reduce the strain on your back and your neck. You should remember to take short breaks and go for a walk as often as possible. Standing up and doing some stretching exercises will help, too!

Quick Fact

Most American teens spend a lot of time on the Internet. Around 87 percent of teens between the ages of 12 and 17 are Internet users. The average teen spends five and a half hours in front of his or her computer every day.

A splint can keep the wrist straight, which eases the pain of carpal tunnel syndrome.

The Expert Says...

"The worst thing about the Internet is the damage it has done to our children's bodies due to ... prolonged sitting at computer stations that are not ergonomically correct for their bodies. We are now seeing injuries in children such as carpal tunnel ... that we used to see only in adults a few years ago."

— Dr. Steven Conway, National Spokesperson for the American Chiropractic Association

You've Got Pain!

Not all aches and pains come from playing sports or from tripping and falling. Some happen over time and can be caused just by surfing the Web. Look at the following labeled diagram to find out more.

EYES

Did you know that the human eye has an easier time looking at objects that are more than 20 feet away? This means that your eyes need to work extra hard to read the text on computer screens. This can make your eyes tired and cause symptoms such as blurred vision and headaches.

NECK

Looking upward at a computer screen for a long period of time can cause temporary cramps or long-term pains in your neck. Some neck problems can appear right away, but others might take years to pop up. Once they arise they can last a lifetime.

WRISTS

A lot of typing can be necessary when talking to friends online or doing homework, but repeating the same motion can tire the wrist and cause permanent damage. Also, most computer mice are designed to fit in the palms of adults' hands. This means that younger peoples' hands must make exaggerated movements in order to move the mouse. This can lead to cramping in the wrist.

BACK

Wearing a heavy backpack isn't the only way that homework can give you a sore back. Leaning forward or slouching at a desk can also cause back strain. Sometimes previous back injuries, such as a sports injury, can be made worse by poor posture at a computer desk.

Take Note

Bad ergonomics comes in at #10. This painful problem can cause damage that lasts a lifetime. Unlike many of the problems on this list, bad ergonomics doesn't affect victims' minds or wallets — it affects their bodies.

- We know that spending too many hours on the Internet can damage your body, but how do you think it could also damage your mind? Explain.

What other health problems can you think of that might arise from too much Internet use?

9 ILLEGAL DOW

Listening to music and watching movies online can be a lot of fun. However, many people don't realize that these activities can also be cybercrimes!

NLOADING

ALSO KNOWN AS: Piracy, stealing, cyber plagiarism

NET NIGHTMARE: Every day, materials are copied from the Internet without the permission of the original creator or the owner.

COMPUTER CRIME–GETTY IMAGES/DAVID MCGLYNN/200112979-001

Has it ever crossed your mind that you, or someone you know, could be an Internet criminal? Well, in the Internet age, it's almost hard not to be! Billions of dollars are lost every year because people are illegally downloading movies and music, plagiarizing original research, and using photographs from the Web without permission.

Many people don't think about the fact that everything on the Web has been created and posted online by somebody else. A person's creations are known as "intellectual property." Intellectual property cannot be reproduced without the owner's permission. Most work on the Web is copyrighted. This means that the creator or owner of the work has to give approval before it is reproduced. But the Internet makes it very hard to protect intellectual property.

Illegally downloading somebody else's work isn't exactly like shoplifting, but it is similar. It's theft — plain and simple.

---

plagiarizing: *using another person's ideas and pretending that they are your own*

ILLEGAL DOWNLOADING

TECH MESS

It's easy to forget that most things on the Internet belong to someone else. Images, artwork, and information that you see online often don't come with a price tag. But this doesn't mean that they're free to copy and use. Illegal downloading can be as easy as a few clicks of the mouse. It can be done by downloading files using programs that don't require a payment, or by copying and pasting images or text. Students who copy and paste information into an essay are guilty of plagiarism.

? Why do you think many people think that what is on the Internet is free for them to take and use as they please?

Quick Fact

In October 2007, Radiohead released their seventh album called *In Rainbows*. Instead of selling it in stores, the band released it as a digital download first. Fans could choose how much they wanted to pay or even download it for free. This had everybody talking! When the CD was released in stores in December 2007, it immediately rose to the top of the charts in both the United Kingdom and the United States.

Quick Fact

The Recording Industry Association of America estimates that illegal downloading causes the economy to lose $12.5 billion and 71,000 jobs every year. This is because fewer CDs than ever are being made and sold. However, some media analysts think that downloading can have positive effects on the music industry. Even though downloading music can cause people to buy fewer CDs, it can also inspire them to check out a concert or buy their favorite band's T-shirt.

SO WHAT?

The Internet has been a wonderful tool for writers, musicians, and visual artists. They can share their work with millions of people within seconds. But there is a downside to this. Artists and the companies that support them are losing billions of dollars. This is because Internet users are stealing their work instead of buying it online or from a store. Not everyone who steals intellectual property is fined or serves jail time — but these consequences are possibilities! Most people who are charged with the theft of intellectual property have no previous criminal record.

FIGHTING BACK!

There are ways that you can take a stand against the theft of intellectual property on the Internet. When downloading music, movies, video games, software, and images, make sure you're doing so from legal Web sites. Paying a small fee to legally download a movie, song, or video isn't necessarily a bad thing. Chances are the quality will be better this way. Don't copy and paste material that you find online without citing your sources. Also, ask your teacher or a librarian if the piece of work you're looking at is part of the public domain. This means that enough time has passed that it is no longer protected by copyright laws and is free for everybody to use.

---

software: *programs that make computers do specific tasks*

The Expert Says...

"Just as stealing property from a store is a crime, stealing intellectual property using the Internet is also illegal. Today, the Internet offers many legitimate and legal ways to pay for video games, music, movies, and software that can be downloaded off the Internet."

— Michael Dubose, Deputy Chief, Computer Crime and Intellectual Property Section, Criminal Division, U.S. Department of Justice

MUSICIANS FIGHT BACK

Read the following quotations from musicians for their views on illegal downloading.

"We really look at it as stealing, because to us it's black and white, either you pay for it or you don't. And you're not paying for it."

— NELLY

"It may seem innocent enough, but every time you illegally download music a songwriter doesn't get paid. And every time you swap that music with your friends a new artist doesn't get a chance. Respect the artists you love by not stealing their music. You're in control. Support music, don't steal it."

— DIXIE CHICKS

"Making an album is a team effort, so when somebody pirates a record, that not only affects the artist, but also the people who worked on it, like coproducers, cowriters, and musicians."

pirates: *reproduces without permission*

— SHAKIRA

"Downloading can be a great way to share music, but downloading music illegally threatens the future of everyone that depends on you for their livelihood. Get music the right way! If you download, do it legally!"

— KEITH URBAN

The Dixie Chicks are against illegal downloading and are taking action to stop it.

Take Note

This nasty crime steals the #9 spot. Though stealing intellectual property online is different from walking into a store and stealing a CD of your favorite artist's music, many people in the music industry would argue it has the same consequences.

- Compare these two types of theft. How are they the same and how are they different?

8 WEB SITE CR

Like tabloid newspapers, Internet sites can make some wild claims! Sometimes it's hard to know what is fact and what is fiction.

EDIBILITY

ALSO KNOWN AS: Disinformation, misleading facts

NET NIGHTMARE: The Internet can be a great source of information, but not everything you read on the Internet is true. In fact, many Web sites contain information that is inaccurate.

With about $50 and some basic computer skills, anybody can launch their own Web site. Sounds like a great deal! However, this means that anybody can post just about anything on the Internet. This makes it very difficult to determine which Web sites are accurate and which ones are not.

Using the Internet to search for information is a huge advantage of the Internet age. You probably use it to find out where the latest movies are playing, check sports scores, and do research for school assignments. It's quick and it's easy. But you wouldn't do a school project with information from an outdated or inaccurate book. The same rules apply to information you find while searching the Web. Unlike newspapers or magazines, most Web sites don't have editors who are always checking the facts.

It's impossible to say just how many Web sites exist on the Internet. This number is changing every second. With thousands of message boards, blogs, and personal Web pages, the Internet is full of mistakes and biased opinions. As a good researcher, it's important to know that you can't always trust what you read.

---

blogs: *personal online journals*
biased: *personal, unreasonable judgments*

WEB SITE CREDIBILITY

TECH MESS

A Web site can be inaccurate for a number of reasons. Some Web sites are hoaxes. They are designed to look like an official Web site, such as one for a well-known organization or company. The creators of these sites are hoping that Internet users will enter their personal information on the site or send money. Other Web sites might provide misleading information, especially if they are trying to sell you products. And some sites might just be plain wrong! Not everyone with a Web site is an expert. The information people post could be only an opinion, or their facts might not be properly researched.

SO WHAT?

Most students prefer to do research on the Internet instead of going to the library. Using incorrect information on a test or in an essay might be a disaster. It could even cause a slump in your grades! Wrong or misleading information can also harm your health. Many adults go online to find answers to their medical problems instead of or before going to a doctor. Wrong information could be more than just frustrating — it could be deadly!

FIGHTING BACK!

When you are trying to decide whether the information on a Web site is accurate, ask yourself some basic questions: Who is responsible for the information on this Web site? Is the author's name and background clearly posted? Where does the Web site come from? Is it a reliable source, such as a university, a government agency, or a trusted media organization? Check to make sure that the information is up to date. Also, try to determine whether the Web site is trying to inform and teach you more about a subject or whether it is trying to persuade you to choose a side of an argument or to buy a product.

When you're looking for news, weather updates, or the latest sports scores, where do you search first for reliable information?

Quick Fact

Thirty-three percent of American youth between the ages of eight and 17 prefer to get information from the Internet instead of over the phone, radio, or television. The majority of students also say that they use the Internet instead of the library for major projects.

The Expert Says...

"The information we consume forms the foundation for our beliefs and our view of the world. It is most important we carefully select the sources of our information and the information we hold to be true."

— Art Exner, Assistant Director of Information Services, University of Regina

LIBRARY STUDENT–ISTOCKPHOTO; ALL OTHER IMAGES–SHUTTERSTOCK

10 9 **8** 7 6

TO TRUST OR NOT TO TRUST

Researching is tough when you don't know which Web sites to trust. Read the following questions and answers for some helpful tips.

Q What are some quick ways to tell whether a Web site is trustworthy?

A Start by looking at the publication date. It is usually found at the bottom of the page. This is a fast way of finding out whether information is outdated. Also, Web site creators are very proud of awards they receive and will likely list them on their Web sites. This will tell you whether a Web site has received a positive response.

? Just as you shouldn't judge a book by its cover, you shouldn't think that a Web site is reliable because it looks official or full of information. What are some tricks that you can use to decide whether a Web site is real or fake?

Q A lot of Web sites seem to be advertising products. Does this mean facts on the Web site might be inaccurate?

A Yes. A lot of Web sites use facts and statistics to persuade you to buy a product. These facts might be right, but they might also be used to stretch the truth to make buyers think they need to make the purchase. Marketers often create "virtual playgrounds" that combine advertising with fun games, flashy graphics, and interesting facts. They might be fun Web sites, but they aren't the best sources for school projects or studying for exams.

Q Can a URL help determine whether a Web site is trustworthy?

A A URL can tell you a lot about a site's origin. A "top-level domain" is found toward the end of a URL, following a period. It is usually made up of two or three letters, and it can be very informative. Here are some examples:

.gov — Symbolizes a Web site for a branch of government
.edu — Symbolizes a Web site for an educational institution, such as a university or college
.org — Symbolizes a Web site for an organization, although this doesn't always mean a site is reputable. Ask your teacher or librarian if you haven't heard of the organization.

You will find that these sites are more likely to be reliable sources of information. They are more trustworthy than Web sites that end in .com or .net., which are often helpful, but their origins are more difficult to track.

URL: *Internet address*

Take Note

The lack of credibility of many Web sites comes in at #8. With one wrong click, computer users might find themselves in a sea of inaccurate information. Like theft of intellectual property, this problem with the Internet affects millions of people. This is especially true as more and more people choose to do research online instead of in a library.

- Why do you think many people prefer to use the Internet to find information instead of reading it in a book?

7 MALWARE

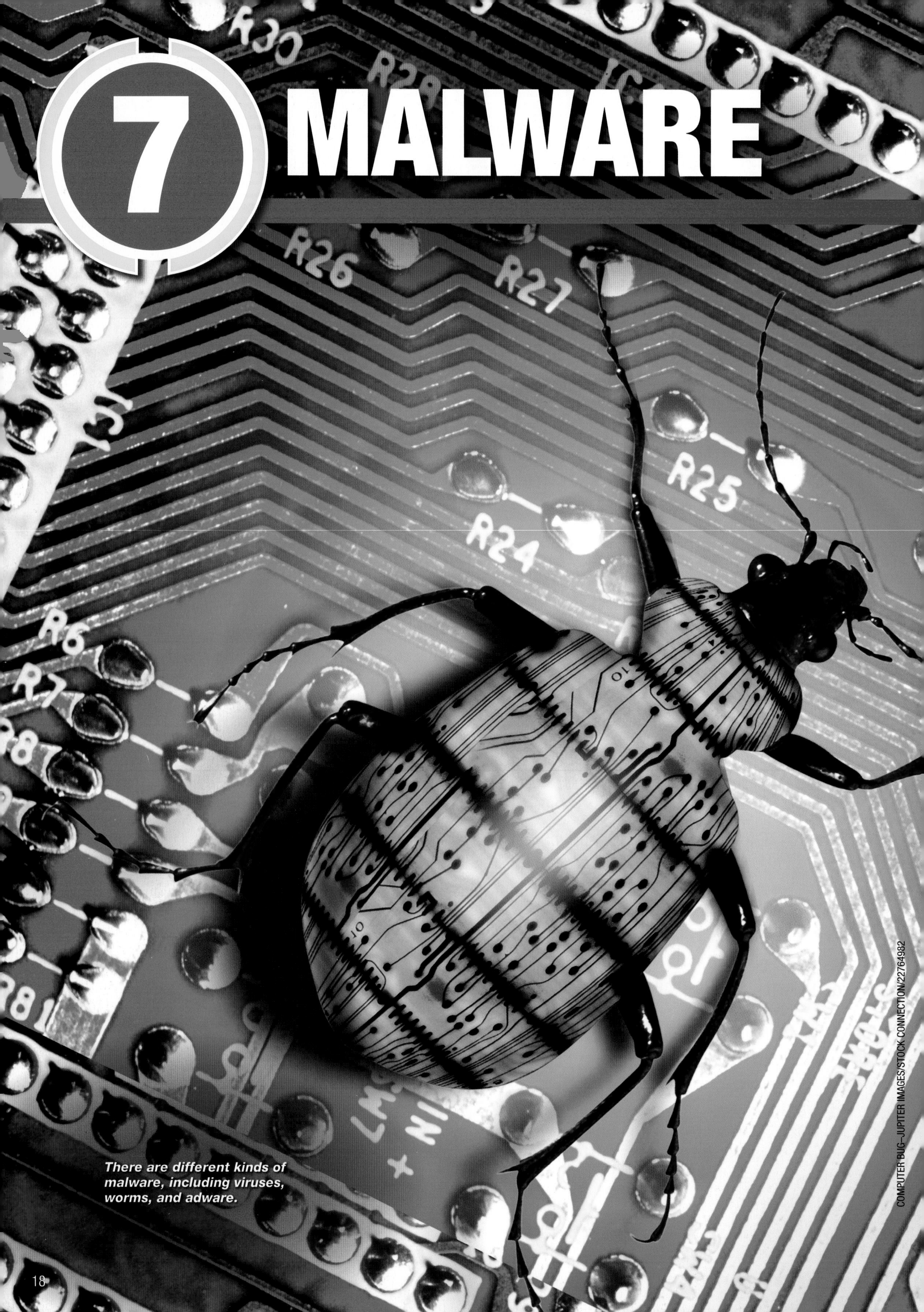

There are different kinds of malware, including viruses, worms, and adware.

COMPUTER BUG–JUPITER IMAGES/STOCK CONNECTION/22764982

ALSO KNOWN AS: Badware, malicious code, malcode

NET NIGHTMARE: These sinister programs are designed to alter or destroy the way a computer works without the computer user's knowledge.

Just as a human can contract a virus, so can a computer! Sure, the symptoms are different and the consequences of a human illness can be much worse, but both can be very frustrating.

A computer virus is a type of malware. Malware, short for malicious software, is designed to damage or destroy the data stored in your computer. Malware comes in many different forms, including Trojan horses, spyware, and worms.

Any one of these harmful programs can be very frustrating if it attacks your personal computer. But just think of the kind of damage that it could cause if it attacked an entire network of computers. Businesses, medical facilities, banks, and government agencies must be very careful that they don't get hit by any type of malware. This means spending a lot of money on extra security measures. State-of-the-art antivirus programs are essential.

---

virus: *program that attaches itself to other programs and documents*
Trojan horses: *programs that look useful but actually cause damage*
spyware: *software that is installed in a computer without the user's knowledge and transmits information about the user's computer activities over the Internet*
worms: *programs that send themselves between computers*

MALWARE

TECH MESS

Computer criminals can easily take the joy out of surfing the Web. They deliberately try to cause damage to computers by unleashing malware. Malware can be attached to an e-mail, a song that you download, or a pop-up advertisement. Some malware can enter a computer without being detected immediately. A sneaky infection can enter your computer like a slow-moving disease. It will creep through your system and destroy whatever is in its path.

SO WHAT?

No matter how many antivirus programs you put on your computer, you're still at risk. Once a form of malware gets into a computer it can cause serious damage, including making the computer run slower than normal or shutting it down altogether. If you notice unusual error messages on your computer, it might be infected. Becoming infected with malware can be more than just frustrating. It can also be expensive! It is estimated that businesses around the world lost $55 billion due to computer viruses in 2003. Fixing a computer can be very expensive, and workers waste valuable time waiting for them to be fixed. Malware can create many problems for a computer user, and it can also mean jail time and hefty fines for the creators of malware.

FIGHTING BACK!

Malware is hidden all over the Web, including e-mails, chat rooms, and music downloading applications. Like illegal downloading, this problem with the Internet affects millions of people. One way to protect yourself is to check your system on a regular basis for corrupt software. This can be done by using a software program that looks for viruses and other malware. It is a good idea to back up all of your computer's data by saving it on a CD, DVD, or external hard drive. This way if your computer crashes you won't lose all of your information. Never open a file that is sent to you by someone you don't know! It might look like something interesting, but you never know where a virus might lurk.

---

hard drive: *device for storing computer data*

If your home computer was infected with a virus, it could be a real disaster! But just imagine what could happen if a virus got into a bank's computer system. What are some reasons that an infection like this would be a major problem?

The Expert Says...

"Criminals ... create viruses and worms to infect computers over the Internet. You can protect your computer by not clicking on Web links in e-mails received from unknown people. You should also run a firewall and up-to-date antivirus software."

— Stefan Saroiu, professor of computer science, University of Toronto

---

firewall: *program designed to protect a computer from unauthorized access*

ALL IMAGES–SHUTTERSTOCK

10 9 8 **7** 6

Computer worms are a form of malware. They can cause a lot of damage! Read the following fact cards to find out more about three of the nastiest computer worms in recent history.

The Melissa Worm

In early 1999, the Melissa worm crept into e-mail contact lists around the world. It sent an infected e-mail, which contained a very destructive file, to 50 people on a victim's contact list. Each time someone opened this file, the worm spread to his or her contact list and the problem got bigger and bigger! It spread so quickly that it prompted major corporations, including Microsoft, to shut down their e-mail programs altogether to stop it from spreading. One strange twist to this worm was that it made its way into existing files on a victim's computers and inserted quotes from a very popular television show — *The Simpsons*!

The ILOVEYOU Worm

This worm was first discovered in May 2000 in Hong Kong. It arrived in e-mail boxes around the world with the subject line "ILOVEYOU." Sounds sweet! Many recipients thought this e-mail was real, so they opened the attached file. It would then overwrite files on their computers. The ILOVEYOU worm also snuck into the victims' e-mail address books and sent the worm out to all their friends! In just one day this love letter spread across the entire world! It infected 10 percent of computers that were connected to the Web. In the end, it caused up to $10 billion in damages.

The Sasser Worm

This worm, which appeared in 2004, was unlike many other malware attacks. Instead of being spread by e-mail, it attacked holes in existing security software. This caused computers to repeatedly crash. It was created by a 17-year-old student in Germany. Sasser was so destructive that the system failures it caused forced airlines to cancel flights. It even blocked satellite communications!

Have you ever encountered malware on your computer? What kind do you think it was? What did you do in order to get rid of it?

Quick Fact

The Sapphire Worm, or the Slammer, broke records in 2003 when it became the fastest-spreading worm in history. It took only 10 minutes to spread to more than 75,000 computers all over the world.

Take Note

We ranked malware #7 on our list. It can infect a computer with just one wrong click. It can come from a complete stranger or from someone you know who has sent it to you unknowingly. Serious computer infections can wipe out hospital records, airport traffic controls, banking facilities, not to mention your personal computer. Computers control much of our daily lives and some malware can really mess things up.

- How might your daily life change if malware destroyed your computer?

6 IDENTITY THE

Identity thieves steal people's money and damage their reputations.

> Scanning...
• Date of Birth: September 27
1526378261
1253617283
7849302843
4378902984
3294594789
• Eye Color: Blue
• Hair Color: Brown
> Identity matched
> Access granted

EYE SCAN AND BINARY CODE–SHUTTERSTOCK

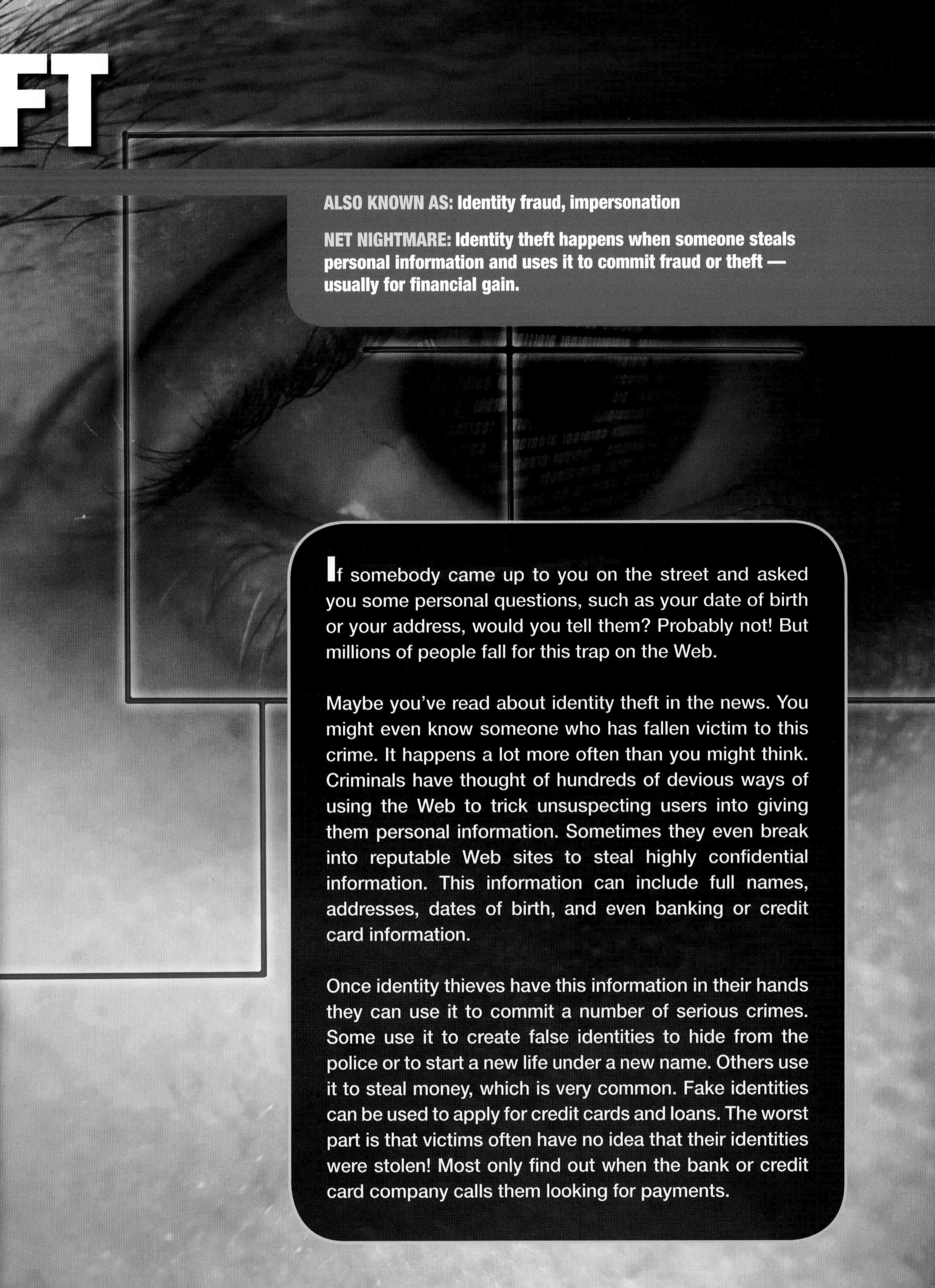

ALSO KNOWN AS: Identity fraud, impersonation

NET NIGHTMARE: Identity theft happens when someone steals personal information and uses it to commit fraud or theft — usually for financial gain.

If somebody came up to you on the street and asked you some personal questions, such as your date of birth or your address, would you tell them? Probably not! But millions of people fall for this trap on the Web.

Maybe you've read about identity theft in the news. You might even know someone who has fallen victim to this crime. It happens a lot more often than you might think. Criminals have thought of hundreds of devious ways of using the Web to trick unsuspecting users into giving them personal information. Sometimes they even break into reputable Web sites to steal highly confidential information. This information can include full names, addresses, dates of birth, and even banking or credit card information.

Once identity thieves have this information in their hands they can use it to commit a number of serious crimes. Some use it to create false identities to hide from the police or to start a new life under a new name. Others use it to steal money, which is very common. Fake identities can be used to apply for credit cards and loans. The worst part is that victims often have no idea that their identities were stolen! Most only find out when the bank or credit card company calls them looking for payments.

IDENTITY THEFT

TECH MESS

Identity theft is making online criminals so much money that they keep coming up with new ways to scam people. "Phishing" (pronounced "fishing") is one way that identity thieves prowl the Internet. This is done by sending official-looking e-mails to a large group of people. Sometimes these e-mails look almost exactly like something a bank or credit card company would send. They might appear to be offering prizes or free gifts. Thieves hope to reel in victims by getting them to type in personal information. Others use "key logging." This technique uses malware to record every letter or number that users type into their computers. This gives thieves easy access to passwords and banking information.

Quick Fact

Most cases of identity theft happen to adults who have credit cards, but this isn't always the case. The Federal Trade Commission received more than 11,600 complaints in 2005 for identity-theft victims who were under the age of 18.

SO WHAT?

Billions of dollars are lost every year because of identity theft. Victims of identity theft can have their entire lives ruined! Some victims find themselves in major debt that they cannot repay. This might leave them with bad credit. This could lead to a poor financial record that makes it difficult to take out student loans or purchase a house in the future. Most victims spend approximately 600 hours trying to rebuild their lives. They also have to pay an average of $2,000 in expenses. This is money that they will never get back!

Online criminals can be forced to pay fines and spend time in jail, but they are often very difficult to catch. Why do you think this is?

FIGHTING BACK!

Experts recommend a number of steps to take so that you and your family don't become victims of identity theft. Avoid filling out forms on the Web that ask for personal information. You never know where that data could end up! This especially includes Web sites that promise great gifts or chances to win contests. Installing fraud-monitoring software helps, too. These programs will tell you whether a Web site is real or not. Any site that does not pass this test could be dangerous.

---

debt: *money owing*
credit: *financial standing*

The Expert Says...

"Ultimately, you cannot prevent identity theft from happening to you. ... You can only reduce your chances."

— Beth Givens, Director of the Privacy Rights Clearinghouse, a project to protect consumers from identity theft

STOLEN LIVES

Identity Thief Finds Easy Money Hard to Resist

An article from *The New York Times*
By Tom Zeller Jr., July 4, 2006

By the time of Shiva Brent Sharma's third arrest for identity theft, at the age of 20, he had taken in well over $150,000 in cash and merchandise in his brief career. After a certain point, investigators stopped counting. ...

Mr. Sharma had figured out how to buy access to stolen credit card accounts online, change the cardholder information, and ... wire money to himself — sometimes using false identities for which he had created pristine driver's licenses. ...

"It's an addiction, no doubt about that," said Mr. Sharma. ...

Much of this unfolded from the basement of a middle-class family home ... at the hands of a high-school student with a knack for problem solving and an inability, even after multiple arrests, to resist the challenge of making a scheme pay off. ...

Mr. Sharma got started with phishing — sending e-mail meant to dupe recipients into revealing their personal or financial data. ...

From the 100,000 phishing e-mails Mr. Sharma sent, investigators say, about 100 recipients were duped into clicking through to the phony ... Web page he created and filling out the form. Mr. Sharma said he did even better, with about 250 to 300 responses. ...

By the summer of 2004, investigators had begun piecing together a string of complaints from ... consumers whose credit card accounts had been hijacked for tens of thousands of dollars in bogus charges ...

---

pristine: *perfect; like new*
dupe: *trick; deceive*
hijacked: *taken control of*
bogus: *not genuine*

Quick Fact

Shiva Brent Sharma was convicted three times for identity theft in just two years. He was sentenced to two to four years in prison for his crimes. As part of his guilty plea, Sharma admitted to stealing personal identity information and credit card numbers, which he used toward purchasing items such as computers and jewelry.

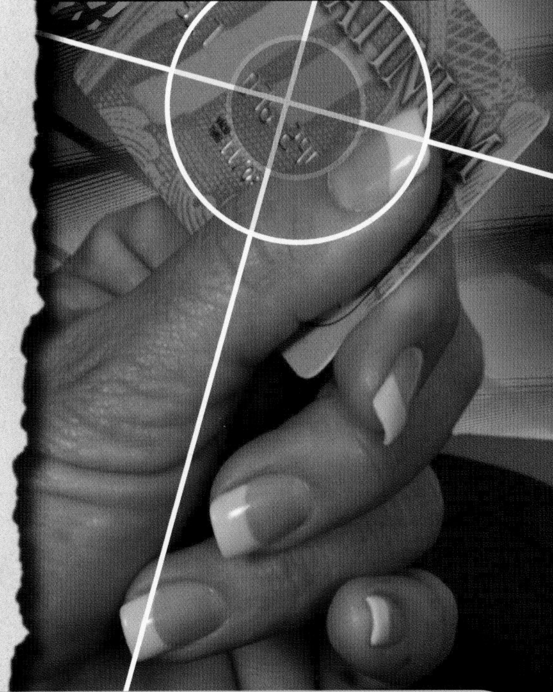

Take Note

We ranked this deceptive deed at #6 on our list. It is a crime that is quickly becoming more common, and it is ruining the lives of millions of victims in the United States alone. Online thieves are out to steal more than just money. They are also trying to steal victims' names and reputations!

- What do you think is worth more — your money or your reputation? Explain.

5 HACKING

Computer hackers can end up spending years in jail for breaking into other people's computers.

HACKERS—© DAVID BRABYN/CORBIS

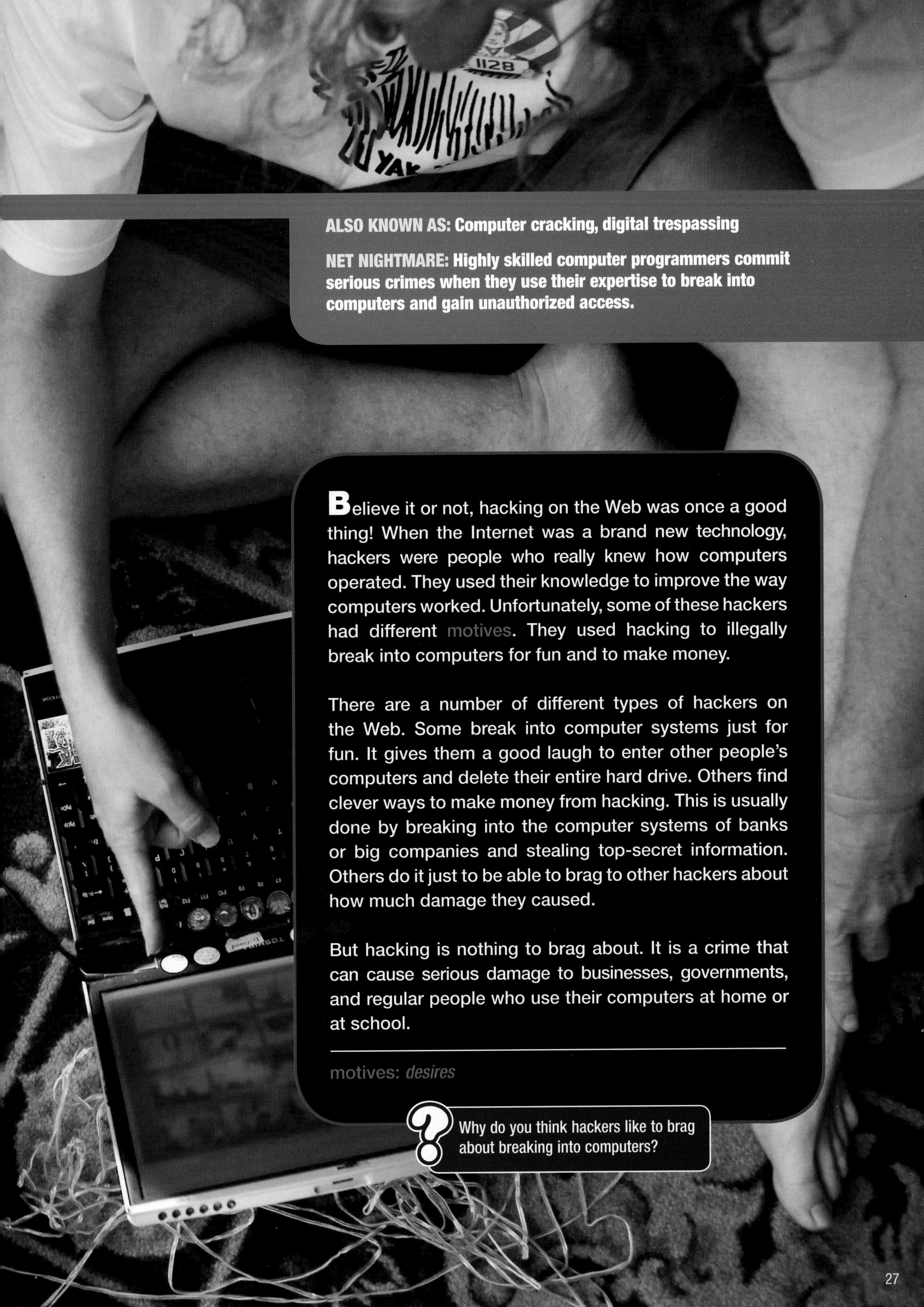

ALSO KNOWN AS: Computer cracking, digital trespassing

NET NIGHTMARE: Highly skilled computer programmers commit serious crimes when they use their expertise to break into computers and gain unauthorized access.

Believe it or not, hacking on the Web was once a good thing! When the Internet was a brand new technology, hackers were people who really knew how computers operated. They used their knowledge to improve the way computers worked. Unfortunately, some of these hackers had different motives. They used hacking to illegally break into computers for fun and to make money.

There are a number of different types of hackers on the Web. Some break into computer systems just for fun. It gives them a good laugh to enter other people's computers and delete their entire hard drive. Others find clever ways to make money from hacking. This is usually done by breaking into the computer systems of banks or big companies and stealing top-secret information. Others do it just to be able to brag to other hackers about how much damage they caused.

But hacking is nothing to brag about. It is a crime that can cause serious damage to businesses, governments, and regular people who use their computers at home or at school.

---

motives: *desires*

Why do you think hackers like to brag about breaking into computers?

HACKING

TECH MESS

Hackers who use their skills for good are known as "white hats." They help businesses find holes in their computer security systems. But "black hats" are a different story. They use their knowledge to disrupt the Web. (These expressions come from old Western movies where the heroes wear white hats and the villains wear black hats.) Hackers can break into banking computers and steal money. They can disrupt airport service after hacking into airport communication systems. They often break into computers and infect them with viruses and worms. Hackers can cause all this trouble by modifying the codes that make up a computer's software. They also use their skills to crack passwords and gain unauthorized access into computers.

? Many hackers serve little time in jail for their crimes. What types of punishment do you think these cyber criminals should face?

SO WHAT?

Hacking has disabled millions of computers around the world. This can be very costly for businesses. The Federal Bureau of Investigation (FBI) estimates that more than $10 billion is lost every year due to computer crimes such as hacking. That's a lot of money! Many hackers are caught by authorities because they boast about what they have done to their friends in online forums. This helps the police track them down and charge them for hacking.

FIGHTING BACK!

In order to fight back against hacking, it is important to change your computer passwords often. Never choose a password like a birth date or a first name. These passwords are too easy for a hacker to crack! The most important thing to do is to install a firewall on your computer. A firewall works like a filter. All information that enters your computer will pass through the firewall first. It will determine whether information is safe enough to pass.

---

boast: *brag; show off*

Quick Fact

One of the youngest hackers was a 14-year-old Canadian boy. His hacking skills caused major problems for some of the world's major Web sites. These included Yahoo!, eBay, and CNN.

The Expert Says...

"As long as there are unsecured computers with interesting stuff on them, there will be hackers. Law enforcement agencies have stepped up their facilities and training programs to meet the demand for computer and network security."

— Dr. Charles C. Palmer, Director of IBM's Privacy Research Institute

ATTACK OF THE CONDOR

Known as the "Condor," Kevin Mitnick was the first hacker to be featured on the FBI's list of most wanted criminals. Even today, he is still considered by many to be the most destructive hacker in history. Read this profile to find out more.

Kevin Mitnick started cracking computer codes and causing minor trouble as a high-school student. This was the beginning of a career headed in the wrong direction. Even after being arrested in 1987 for computer invasion, he still couldn't give up the rush he felt when hacking.

By the 1990s, he could break into just about any computer network, steal credit card information, steal software, and alter computer codes to cause major computer meltdowns! He used the data that he stole from computers to create false identities. Over 13 years, Mitnick broke into the computer systems of at least 35 major companies. These companies estimate that Mitnick's hacking skills cost them approximately $300 million. He did this by spending 11 or 12 hours a day at his computer, altering computer codes.

Mitnick felt little remorse for his crimes. He even said, "It was a big game to me. I was just having a blast!" But his fun came to an end in 1995 when the FBI caught up with him. It had spent two years searching for him! Mitnick's mistake was hacking into the computer of a computer specialist who was equally as talented at hacking. The computer specialist, named Tsutomu Shimomura, used his superior skills to help the FBI track Mitnick down.

Mitnick pleaded guilty in 1995. He spent five years in federal prison. Once released, he was not allowed to use a computer connected to the Internet until 2003. Today he uses his hacking skills for good. He has his own company that specializes in computer security!

---

remorse: *regret; guilt*

Kevin Mitnick

Take Note

We ranked hackers at #5. Unlike identity thieves, these criminals commit many different crimes. They steal money, government files, business secrets, and personal identities. They can also spread malware.

- Compare hackers with other criminals on our list. Who do you think poses the greatest amount of danger to computer users? Explain.

4 SCAMMING

Computer users log on to popular online auctions looking for a great deal. But sometimes these great deals are too good to be true.

COMPUTER HEADACHE–© FOTOSTUDIO FM/ZEFA/CORBIS

ALSO KNOWN AS: Hoaxing, scheming

NET NIGHTMARE: This illegal behavior is done with only one purpose in mind — to steal money from unsuspecting Internet users!

Have you ever heard the saying "it's too good to be true"? Well, chances are, if you find a deal on the Internet that seems too good to be true, it probably is! Online crooks steal from unsuspecting users, tricking them into giving money by using a number of different phony schemes.

Unfortunately, with so many people buying and selling items online, many Internet users become victims of scamming. Scammers make users think they are getting great deals for their money. With authentic-looking e-mails or flashy Web sites, scammers lure people in by telling them they've won a prize or made the highest bid on an online auction. But actually they haven't won anything, and their great deal never materializes!

By the time someone realizes they've been scammed, it's too late. Chances are they've already sent the scammer some money or some personal information that can lead to identity theft.

---

schemes: *plans; plots*

SCAMMING

TECH MESS

Not all Internet users can tell the difference between a real deal and a scam. This is because scammers are good at what they do! Some scammers create fake profiles on Web sites such as eBay and pretend to have products to sell. People buy these products and send scammers their money.

Unfortunately, some scammers try to profit from tragedy. This is done by creating fake charities and asking people to donate money online. Of course, this money doesn't get to the people who need it. The Internet has become the newest and easiest way to rip people off!

Online scamming has been called a "faceless crime." What do you think this means?

SO WHAT?

Online scams are illegal, but the problem is that it's very difficult to catch some scammers. This is because it's easy for them to remain anonymous. Scammers are often successful because hacking is a low cost business to operate, and there are millions of computer users to prey on. Like victims of identity theft, scamming victims often don't get back the money they've lost.

FIGHTING BACK!

The best way for Internet users to avoid becoming victims of scamming is to question everything on the Internet. This means researching Web sites' policies regarding scamming. Some Web sites will reimburse customers' money if their products never arrive. Follow the same steps that you take when determining whether a Web site is credible and real or just a look-alike. Internet users can also go online to the Better Business Bureau's Web site. The Better Business Bureau is an organization that provides feedback on companies, which can help separate the good companies from the bad.

reimburse: *repay; refund*

Quick Fact

One of the longest jail terms for Internet auction fraud was 12 years. This was for a man from the United States who was convicted of scamming $100,000 from 268 victims.

Make sure that a charity organization is authentic before you make a donation.

The Expert Says...

"I tell myself that if something online seems too good to be true — like a once-in-a-lifetime deal or a quick way to earn lots of money — it probably is! This helps me to always be wise with my interactions in cyberspace, which keeps me, my identity and personal information, and my money safe and secure."

— Sameer Hinduja, Assistant Professor, Department of Criminology and Criminal Justice, Florida Atlantic University

SAMEER HINDUJA–COURTESY OF SAMEER HINDUJA; KATRINA FLOOD–ISTOCKPHOTO; ALL OTHER IMAGES–SHUTTERSTOCK

FOR A GOOD CAUSE?

When tragedies happen, many people want to do what they can to help. This often means donating money to charities. Unfortunately, some scammers take advantage of this. Read the following fact chart to find out more.

TSUNAMI

On December 26, 2004, an earthquake caused a tsunami that killed more than 200,000 people in Sri Lanka, India, Indonesia, Thailand, and Malaysia. In 2005, police arrested a man named Matthew Schmieder. They suspected that he sent out 800,000 e-mails asking people to donate money to tsunami victims. Instead of donating the money to these victims, he used the money to pay his bills. Police think that Schmieder's scam was one of many similar scams. Most of these scammers used phishing e-mails that looked real.

tsunami: *large wave usually caused by an underwater earthquake*

Tsunami refugees in Indonesia

HURRICANE KATRINA

In 2005, Hurricane Katrina killed almost 2,000 people and left many more thousands homeless. After the tragedy, a man from Florida named Gary Kraser created a Web site for a fake charity. He promised that all the money he raised would go toward airlifting emergency supplies and helping sick children in New Orleans. Police say that the scam earned Kraser $40,000. He even used his Web site to tell fake stories about the horrible things that he saw in New Orleans while supposedly delivering the supplies. In the end, Kraser was sentenced to 21 months in prison.

Hurricane Katrina damaged much of the city of New Orleans

Take Note

Scamming is the #4 worst thing about the Internet. Though there are more victims of malware attacks, scammers steal people's money by taking advantage of their trust. They are also often much more difficult to catch.

- Do you agree with our decision to put online scamming ahead of malware? Explain.

3 INTERNET ADD

Playing online games for hours at a time can be a sign of Internet addiction.

INTERNET GAMER–GETTY IMAGES/COLORBLIND IMAGES/200559149-009

ICTION

ALSO KNOWN AS: Internet Addiction Disorder (IAD), Internet dependency

NET NIGHTMARE: Using the Internet too much can lead to addiction, which can cause health, relationship, and financial problems.

With so many fun things to do on the Web, some people just can't seem to log off. These excessive online users are suffering from a condition known as Internet Addiction Disorder (IAD).

Internet addicts start off using the Web like everyone else. The problem is that once they start, they can't stop! The Internet takes over their lives. Addicts perform worse at work or in school. This is because they spend their time surfing the Web when they should be resting or studying. Often their relationships suffer, too. This is because Internet addicts spend more time online than with their friends and families.

Internet addicts go online to chat with friends and they just can't stop. They shop online and spend all of their money. They also play online games that never end — until one day they realize they're hooked. Over time, Internet addicts will begin to suffer from a lack of sleep and exercise. As with anyone with an addiction, Internet addicts need to realize that they have a problem — before it's too late.

INTERNET ADDICTION

TECH MESS

Reports released in recent years have confirmed that Internet addiction is a growing problem. It is estimated that five to 10 percent of Internet users will become addicted. People of all ages can become hooked on online activities. These include instant messaging, multiplayer games, and talking in chat rooms. Unfortunately, many people do not seek help for Internet addiction because they are in denial. Signs that someone is addicted to the Internet include sacrificing food or sleep to spend time online.

SO WHAT?

Once users become addicted to the Internet, other parts of their lives begin to suffer. Internet addicts spend so much time online that they neglect their friends and family. Some people with IAD even lose their jobs because they spend their time surfing the Web when they should be working. One calculation shows that American businesses lose almost $800 billion per year due to employees who waste time at work. Their biggest time waster is the Internet!

denial: *inability to admit the truth*

Quick Fact

In 2005, a couple in the United Kingdom was sentenced to three months in jail for neglecting their children due to an addiction to online gaming.

FIGHTING BACK!

There are some ways that IAD sufferers can fight back against their addiction. They should set a goal and stick to it! This means setting aside a predetermined amount of time for using the Internet. Using a timer can be helpful. When the timer goes off, so does the computer, no excuses! Some counselors specialize in treating severe cases of IAD. They help people of all ages put a stop to their Internet addictions.

predetermined: *set; planned*

Do you think you could tell whether you or someone you knew was addicted to the Internet? What signs would you look for?

The Expert Says...

"It's a bigger and bigger problem. ... [Youth with Internet addictions] aren't developing social skills or academic skills. It seriously affects their grades, which will affect their future [when] they apply to school."

— Joanne Teliszewski, high-school guidance counselor

Quick Fact

Did you know that there is a camp in Germany for kids who are addicted to the Internet? Officials estimate that Germany has close to one million Internet addicts. This is about three percent of the population.

CAUGHT IN THE WEB

A newspaper article from
The Orange County Register
By Katherine Nguyen, January 28, 2007

Thirty seconds. That's how much time Brian Alegre allowed himself for a bathroom break before rushing feverishly back to his computer video game.

The fear of … losing the battle for his team or, worse, being outranked in points by another player compelled the … teenager to guzzle energy drinks and stay glued to his computer for 15 hours straight.

"In the summer, I basically didn't shower or brush my teeth," said Alegre, 19. "I didn't realize it at the time, but yeah, I guess I was addicted." …

With eight million subscribers, [World of Warcraft] is one of the world's most popular MMORPGs — massive multiplayer online role-playing games. Players go adventuring together to defeat monsters, complete quests, and acquire loot. …

After playing 15 to 20 hours a day for nearly four months, Alegre's breaking point came when he realized he might not graduate from high school.

"I had the whole year to do my senior project, which is a requirement to graduate, but I was too busy playing the game," Alegre said. "So three weeks before it was due, I quit cold turkey."

Those who quit report intense, physical withdrawal symptoms and feelings of guilt for deserting fellow players. …

Alegre is playing again and makes it a point to spend more time away from his computer. … "I'll play about two hours or so now, …" he said. "But I'm done being burnt out."

cold turkey: *instantly; all at once*

Have you ever spent long periods of time surfing the Web when you really should have been doing schoolwork? What happened in the end?

World of Warcraft display at the Electronic Entertainment Expo in Los Angeles, California

Take Note

This serious problem with the Internet is #3 on our list. Some Internet addicts need to seek professional help to overcome their addictions. Internet addiction can be so severe that users sacrifice their own health and time with loved ones in order to stay online longer.

- What other types of technology could someone become addicted to? Compare these to Internet addiction.

5 4 **3** 2 1

CYBERBULLYI

MOUSE BULLIES–SHUTTERSTOCK

Victims of cyberbullying can feel helpless when they don't know who is sending them nasty e-mails or instant messages.

ALSO KNOWN AS: Electronic bullying, online victimization

NET NIGHTMARE: The Web can be a scary place where teasing, threatening, and vicious rumors are too common.

The Web can be used to spread information at lightning speed. This is great when it comes to breaking news, but the Internet can also be used to spread lies and rumors. Using the Internet to threaten or intimidate others is known as cyberbullying.

Cyberbullying can be a problem in chat rooms and e-mails, and it can happen over instant messaging programs. Tactics can be similar to traditional methods used by schoolyard bullies, such as name-calling or physical threats. They can also include new kinds of terrible tactics, such as doctoring photos or impersonating others in chat rooms.

This type of bullying often goes unnoticed by parents and teachers. This is because many parents are not as computer-savvy as their children. Also, teachers find online conflicts far more difficult to detect than physical bullying because they are less visible to those outside the conflict. The problem is that cyberbullying can be just as hurtful.

CYBERBULLYING

TECH MESS

Imagine that someone is bullying you online. All you have to do is turn off your computer, right? It's not quite that simple. Cyberbullying isn't like traditional bullying where a bully and victim meet face-to-face. Even after a victim logs off, a bully can continue to spread his or her mean messages across cyberspace. And many victims don't always know who is spreading vicious rumors or sending unpleasant or cruel messages. Instant messenger programs, e-mail, and chat rooms usually lack supervision. Girls in their final years of high school are the most likely victims of cyberbullying.

SO WHAT?

Victims of cyberbullying can feel shame and embarrassment. They can also experience depression and rage. Cyberbullies can face severe consequences. It is illegal to repeatedly communicate with someone in a way that makes them fear for their safety. Cyberbullies can also be guilty of libel. This means they are guilty of injuring another person's reputation in writing, without cause.

FIGHTING BACK!

The problem of cyberbullying is spreading faster than you can say "World Wide Web!" Many schools are fighting back by writing policies that include tough consequences for bullies, such as detentions or expulsions. Educating students on the issue from a young age is also very important. Most experts suggest that victims of cyberbullying should not respond to any taunts. This might just make the problem worse. Luckily, most chat rooms and online messaging programs have functions that allow victims to block messages from people who are causing harm.

Quick Fact

Research shows that most kids who are bullied online don't tell their parents, teachers, or other adults because they are afraid they will lose their computer privileges. This means that the online harassment can go on for months without being reported.

? What do you think are some consequences that students who are cyberbullies should face?

The Expert Says...

"Cyberbullying can be a very harmful form of online aggression because the victim often feels powerless against hurtful and repeated attacks from people who they may or may not know. And because more and more kids are using the Internet, cyberbullying will likely increase in the years to come, unless kids and adults alike take a stand against it."

— Justin Patchin, Assistant Professor of Criminal Justice, University of Wisconsin

A VICTIM'S STORY

October 10, 2002
CBC News

This article tells the story of David Knight, a high-school student who was forced to leave his school due to cyberbullying.

David Knight … was teased, taunted, and punched for years. But the final blow was the humiliation he suffered every time he logged onto the Internet. Someone had set up an abusive Web site about him that made life unbearable. …

"Anyone with a computer can see it," says David. "And you can't get away from it." …

In David's case, the Web site about him had been active for several months before a classmate told him about it. …

"I went there and sure enough there's my photo on this Web site saying 'Welcome to the Web site that makes fun of Dave Knight' and just pages of hateful comments directed at me and everyone in my family." …

Along with the Web site, there were nasty e-mails too. …

"It's a cowardly form of bullying," says [David's mother] Nancy Knight. "It's like being stabbed in the back by somebody (and) you have no way of ever finding out who they are, or defending yourself against the words they say." …

"After this bullying started, he began withdrawing completely, isolating himself from everyone," she says. …

When David's parents learned of the Web site about him, they asked police to investigate, to try and find out who was behind it and have it removed from the Web. But the site stayed up. …

Eventually the Knight family did get [the Internet service company] to take down the Web site about David. But it wasn't easy. It took seven months of messaging, phone calls, and the family thinks, the threat of legal action before it was removed. …

David is now trying to recover from the bullying and beginning to realize his dream. He's learning to fly, hoping to become a fighter pilot in the Canadian Armed Forces. David's starting to soar beyond the nightmare delivered to him by the new technology that, now, all of our children have access to.

---

isolating: *detaching; removing*

Quick Fact

In a 2006 study, around one-third of youth reported that they've experienced cyberbullying. Almost five percent claimed they were afraid for their safety.

Take Note

Cyberbullying comes in at #2 on our list. Though bullying has been a problem in schools for generations, cyberbullying is a whole new problem! Unlike victims of hacking or identity theft, those who face cyberbullying often choose not to report the crime.

- What are some reasons that you think this crime might go unreported? What do you think people who face cyberbullies should do?

1 ONLINE PRE

The Internet can be a scary place when you don't know who is on the other end of an online chat.

DATORS

ALSO KNOWN AS: Cyberstalkers

NET NIGHTMARE: Criminals use the Internet to contact young people and trick them into meeting outside the chat room.

You've probably been told by your parents and teachers that you shouldn't talk to strangers. Well, the Internet has made this danger more common. If you've ever spent time in a chat room or on a message board, then you've definitely been talking to strangers.

Even though many of the people you meet on the Internet seem harmless, there is a group of very dangerous users called predators who stalk the cyber world. They use the Internet to take advantage of young people. Predators search the Internet for potential victims who are looking for someone to talk to. These masters of deception create false identities to scam young people into chatting with them. In reality, they could be gathering victims' personal information and trying to find out where they live or how to convince them to meet outside the chat room.

This problem with the Internet might be more common than you think. One study showed that around 30 percent of teens who use the Internet have talked about meeting someone who they have only met online.

ONLINE PREDATORS

TECH MESS

Online predators use the Internet to contact others, usually children or young people. They use chat rooms, instant messages, e-mails, and discussion boards. Predators use lies and tricks to fool their victims. Some predators lure victims by pretending to be young people themselves. They do this by naming the latest music, movies, and hobbies that young people might want to chat about. Others try to build a level of trust with their victims. This is done by showing a lot of attention, kindness, and understanding as they talk online.

Quick Fact

Many young women between the ages of 13 and 17 report posting personal information on the Internet. This includes 72 percent who have posted their real age; 70 percent who have posted photos or videos of themselves; 48 percent who have posted the city they live in; and seven percent who have included their cell phone numbers.

SO WHAT?

Using the Internet to contact minors online can be illegal, but this doesn't stop predators. Online predators can land in jail or be sent to rehabilitation programs for their crimes. Predators who target underage victims face lengthy prison sentences. This is because most states have laws to protect youth from online predators. Victims are often left with guilt, regret, and a difficulty trusting others.

What do you think can be done to help victims of online predators recover from their experience?

FIGHTING BACK!

Your best defense against Internet predators is to be very aware of who you're chatting with. This means only using chat rooms and instant messages to talk to family and friends, and never to people you don't know. Never give out your name, phone number, or any other personal information to strangers online. The same rule applies when it comes to photographs. You can post pictures for your friends to see, but use security features to ensure that other Internet users can't take a look. The best way to fight back against online predators is to refuse to meet face to face with anyone whom you've met online. Let a parent or teacher know if someone is pressuring you to meet.

---

rehabilitation: *treatment or therapy to help a person avoid committing the same crime in the future*

The Expert Says...

"Remember that the Internet is a public place, which means that nothing is truly private. Online predators are looking for victims, don't be one."

— Judy Foy, constable, National Exploitation Coordination Centre, Canada

TRICKS OF THE TRADE

The following online chat might seem pretty harmless, but even a casual conversation can lead to trouble. Online predators use tricks when talking to young people.

Grlz_Rule1: We won our soccer game today! 

B_ball_boy13: Wicked! What's your team's name?

Grlz_Rule1: I play for the Tillson TireCity Tigers.

B_ball_boy13: Sweet, I play soccer too, even though basketball is my favorite sport.

B_ball_boy13

Grlz_Rule1: I'm a forward, #7. What position do you play?

B_ball_boy13: We haven't started playing yet this year. It's still too cold in northern Michigan. But when we do I'll try out for the goalie position.

Grlz_Rule1: Wow it's still cold there? I live in FL not far from Tampa and we've been playing for like six weeks.

B_ball_boy13: I can't wait till we start up. The first tryouts are this weekend and then my age group plays Monday nights.

Grlz_Rule1: Wicked! I play on Monday nights, too!

Quick Fact

Many teens communicate with strangers online. Most do so using instant messaging (54 percent), e-mail (50 percent), and chat rooms (45 percent).

What Grlz_Rule1 doesn't realize is that she fell for some of B_ball_boy13's tricks:

- B_ball_boy13 asked simple questions, but gathered specific answers. He now knows where she lives and where she will be next Monday evening. He even knows what team she plays for and her jersey number.
- B_ball_boy13 used a fake picture. This helped to convince Grlz_Rule1 that he was 13. He is really 43!
- This online predator also built his relationship with Grlz_Rule1 by acting interested in her hobbies.
- B_ball_boy13 uses words such as "wicked" and "sweet" to help convince Grlz_Rule1 that he is much younger than he is.

Take Note

Online predators sneak in at #1. Unlike other crimes where the consequences are primarily financial, online predators can cause great emotional and physical harm to their victims. As with hacking and identity theft, this crime can land a criminal in jail.

- How would you warn your friends about the dangers of online predators?

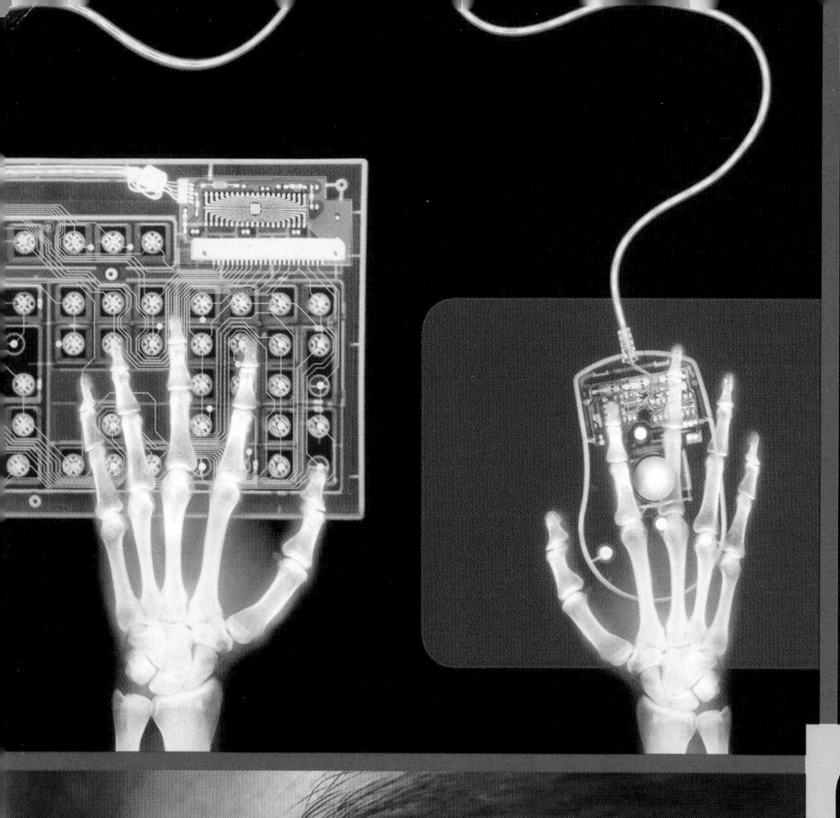

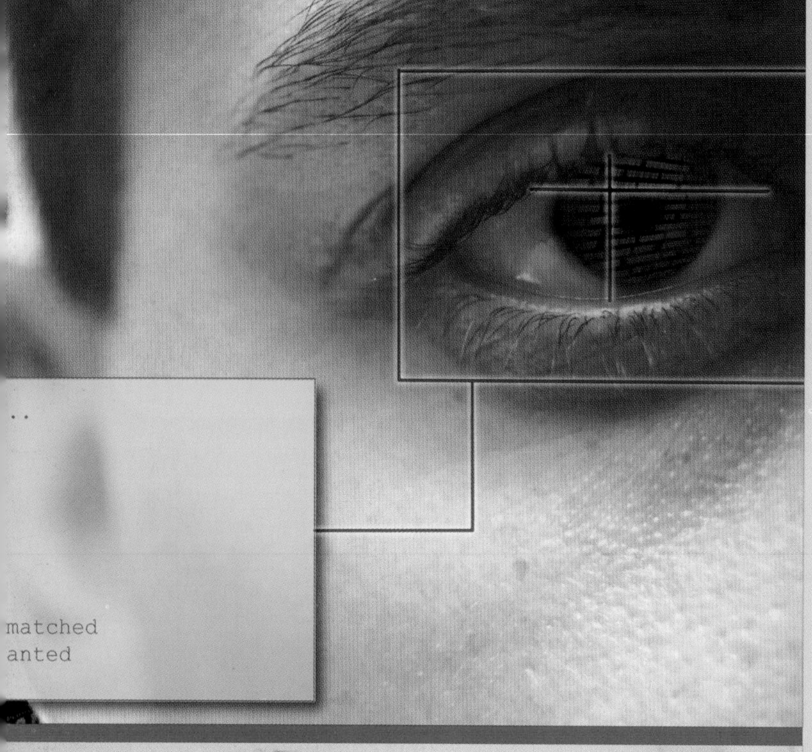

We Thought ...

Here are the criteria we used in ranking the 10 worst things about the Internet.

The problem:

- Happens to millions of people
- Can be difficult to prevent
- Has serious, often legal, consequences
- Causes great damage to a computer
- Can put computer users at a physical risk
- Can happen to all computer users
- Can be difficult to catch
- Can be difficult to fix
- Can be very expensive to computer users and businesses

What Do You Think?

1. Do you agree with our ranking? If you don't, try ranking these worst things about the Internet yourself. Justify your ranking with data from your own research and reasoning. You may refer to our criteria, or you may want to draw up your own list of criteria.

2. Here are three other problems about the Internet that we considered but in the end did not include in our top 10 list: spamming, lost productivity, violent online games.
   - Find out more about these problems. Do you think they should have made our list? Give reasons for your response.
   - Are there other problems with the Internet that you think should have made our list? Explain your choices.

Index